ARE YOU ONE IN A MILLION?

A HUMOROUS LOOK AT THE STATISTICS WHICH MAKE US SPECIAL!

Peter Hewkin

*"Any book without a mistake in it has had
too much money spent on it"*
Sir William Collins, publisher

ARE YOU
ONE IN A
MILLION
?

A HUMOROUS LOOK AT THE
STATISTICS WHICH MAKE US SPECIAL!

Peter Hewkin

ff&f

For Poppy and Tom

Are You One in a Million?
Discover Your Uniqueness Factor
By
Peter Hewkin

Published by
Facts, Figures & Fun, an imprint of
AAPPL Artists' and Photographers' Press Ltd.
Church Farm House, Wisley, Surrey GU23 6QL
info@ffnf.co.uk www.ffnf.co.uk
info@aappl.com www.aappl.com

Sales and Distribution
UK and export: Turnaround Publisher Services Ltd.
orders@turnaround-uk.com

A catalogue record for this book is available from the
British Library.

ISBN 13: 9781904332558
ISBN 10: 1904332552

Design (contents and cover): Malcolm Couch
mal.couch@blueyonder.co.uk

Printed in China by Imago Publishing
info@imago.co.uk

Contents

Celebrities Featured:

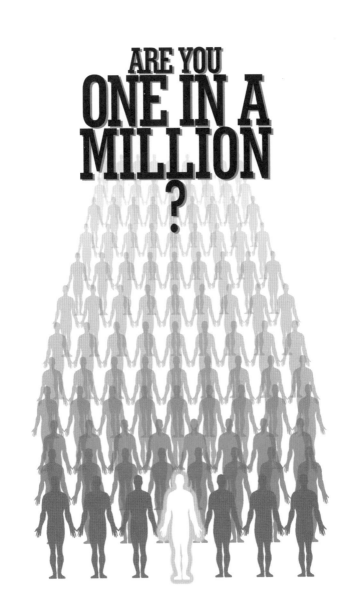

Are You
One in a Million?

Have you ever wondered if there is another bus driver with 5 O-levels who lives in a listed building, plays cricket every weekend and has been to the top of Kilimanjaro? Or whatever achievements fit you personally?

Well now you can find out

By discovering EXACTLY

**"how few people have done
the same things you have"**

This book is *not* about superstars or celebrities and it is unlikely to get you into the Guinness Book of Records (at least I don't think it will).

It *is* about discovering exactly how special *you* are as an individual (but in a fun kind of way).

**'How can I be special if I am not in one of the
groups you just mentioned?'**

Well you will soon find out - I will show you that you may be special in the manner of that old fashioned phrase,

"One in a Million"

And even if you don't quite make it, I feel sure you will still be surprised at just how special you are (And have a reason to try something new...)

We have all been told we're special or unique.

Your mum probably told you, but that doesn't count.

Scientists use this phrase when they discuss psychology or the brain, educationalists use it in discussing children and teaching - but they just mean that our brains and bodies are not the same as anyone else's.

Well so what?

If I just wanted to know that I was unique in such a specific and even (dare I say it?) trivial way, I could easily just prove it by saying I was the only person born on a certain date at a specific time in a particular hospital from a given mother and that would just about do it.

But then I'm 'unique' – in precisely the SAME way that everyone else is.

Now isn't that **exactly** what you and I **don't** want to feel?

In this book you will find out how 'unique' you really are because of

What you can do, have done or are.

I have tried to ensure each possible achievement is

nontrivial in the sense that it could only apply to some people by virtue of 'an accident of place/time of birth' (although I have included a section on your 'Biological Self' as it contains many characteristics by which we define ourselves. It is up to you whether you choose to include these in your own Uniqueness Factor or not).

As you read my book, you will see many of the achievements require some (albeit perhaps small) effort on your part to do/have done it *and yet almost* everything could be done by most people given enough effort on their part (and perhaps a little luck); but *only* if they made the effort –

And that's the whole point – not everyone does.

So when you have finished reading I am confident that you will be amazed at what you have found out about your own special 'uniqueness' and will be able to claim – with genuine justification – that you are truly one in a million (or at least very nearly). Meanwhile I want you to have some 'serious' fun discovering more about yourself than you probably believed possible.

So Read on and Good luck finding your Uniqueness Factor (UF)

Oh and before I forget - A few of the things are probably too weird to actually aim for, but you never know.....

How do I find my 'Uniqueness Factor (UF)'?

First find a pen or pencil and a piece of paper
and a simple calculator

. . . . .

Then look in the contents list

. . . . .

Find something you are/have done or can do*
(Be as honest as you can)

. . . . .

Jot down the likelihood that someone has done it
in the Personal Logs provided throughout this book

. . . . .

Do the whole exercise again and carry on until
you have your 'Best Five' and record these
at the end of this book

Now the fun begins

*You may have to accept a level of achievement that does not
match exactly – please use your best judgment and choose the
nearest similar category or estimate extra categories as
explained later in the book.

Multiply the five 'big numbers' to get the likelihood
that anyone has done those things *you* have –
this is your **Uniqueness Factor**
(see the next section if you need help with this)

And when you've done it all copy and complete
one of the Certificates of Personal Achievement
found at the end of the book to 'prove'

Only one person in (insert UF) has/is ....
and .... and .... and............
and ....!

Celebrate your amazement with
an appropriate beverage

Try it out on your friends and relatives
who can also complete a Certificate

Pass it on

And if you **do** achieve the 'highly coveted' soubriquet
of being **"one in a million"** then you know you
may be amongst **only 40 or so adults in the whole
country** who have done those five things – any
other Uniqueness Factor can easily be figured out
using this as a baseline.

Oh, and a **Uniqueness Factor of greater than 1
in 40 million** means you are quite possibly the only
person in the country to have done all those things.

But Don't Stop There

Try a different combination
And see what you can score with other
categories.

Repeat this as many times as you like.

You may just want to find that you are the only left-handed owner of a Dalmatian dog who also lives in a thatched cottage and drives a car older than you are: if so fine...

But just maybe
there are more meaningful
categories to aspire to...

How to do the Calculations

Let us assume you have found five categories of achievement that you have recorded in the relevant places in this book – now you want to know what to do with them.

Let's say the probabilities are:

1 in 5
1 in 20
1 in 4
1 in 100
and
1 in 15

First of all ignore the '1 in whatever' bits and just write down the whole numbers like so:

5   20   4   100   15

Now write down the number of zeros and then cross them off like so:

5   2   4   1   15   with three zeros

Multiply these simpler numbers

5 x 2 x 4 x 1 x 15 = 600

and then put the zeros on at the end:

600 + 000 giving 600,000

And therefore you have a Uniqueness factor of

One in 600,000 people!

(or, if your calculator can cope with that many noughts simply multiply 5 x 20 x 4 x 100 x 15)

You will also need this to calculate the UF for your favourite celebrities to be found throughout the book.

Some More Things to Do

1. Make a plan to try some of the other categories at a future date and improve your 'Uniqueness Factor'. I have included some 'advice' on how this might be done throughout the book – sometimes this involves contacting the relevant organisation, otherwise the suggestion might be rather more 'tongue in cheek'! **Some are potentially dangerous!** Just don't blame me for getting yourself into trouble if you try to do them!

2. Include the low probability categories in your CV for your next job application and impress the interviewer.

3. What is the point in doing 100 or more things just to say you did them? OK so it's lots of fun doing them if you ever get the chance and even more fun telling your friends you did. But why not get those books off the shelf again and increase the fun and self-satisfaction by re-reading them alongside this book and seeing what else you would like to try?

4. As mentioned let your friends, relatives, spouse or significant other try it for himself or herself.

Best of Luck Again!

The Celebrities Sections

Now I know I said earlier that this book was not about celebrities, but about YOU. Well, dotted around the book you will find examples of celebrities (my definition and choice – not necessarily yours) who have done some of the things in the list, and examples of others who have done a combination of things – other than the ones for which they are actually famous.

So now you can see how special they might have been on a selection of factors other than the particular talents for which they are best known.

I have given you the chance to actually calculate the Uniqueness Factors of your favourite celebrities – these are both for your amusement and comparative edification. You might even find you are more 'unique' than some very famous people.

Well, sort of…

Questions Regarding the Data

Now you may ignore this bit until later if you want, but it will explain some of the underlying assumptions, statistical analysis techniques and so on that I used in this book.

The first question you might ask is "How did I get the numbers?"

I have made a serious effort to assess and confirm the probabilities or 'likelihoods' that you will read about, but as with statistics in general, there is always room for error.

In particular when I have given a 'likelihood factor' it is out of the recognised United Kingdom adult (over 16 years old in most instances) population of approximately 40 million people, rather than all living people for better accuracy – most of the things in the book are not likely to have been done yet by younger people.

For the reader's further information, calculations have been based on figures of 21 million homes and 30 million vehicles in the United Kingdom at the present time. Many of the figures I have given were derived from the references given later in the book. Most of these are recognised National Statistics sources, governing bodies or the websites of the institutions, clubs, associations, etc., involved. However in some cases data still varied from source to source by a factor of ten or more even when all were equally 'reliable', hence it was often necessary to integrate data from many sources to find one acceptable value!

Even where good data existed it was often necessary to extrapolate in order to produce the best possible data from annual returns and so on e.g. tourism and passenger figures were mostly based on current travel rates and not on long term trends or lifestyle surveys.

As for the rest, I would not wish to claim that some of my figures are much more than 'ball park' values but nevertheless as far as I could I have ensured these are as accurate as possible.

If you know of better values you can email me via the publishers at info@ffnf.co.uk

You may also notice a lot of seemingly obvious categories don't appear – that is precisely the point. When something – having a bank account, being right handed (as opposed to left handed), and so on, is so likely that the probability is much greater than 50% i.e. not even 1 in anything, I have often not used it. It would be pointless in the 'uniqueness factor' to multiply by this number, as only a little thought will show.

What I have done in many cases is include the much less likely case that you HAVE NOT done it.

So, if you can't find it in the book either I just didn't get around to locating the probability (or didn't think of it) or it is unexceptional and therefore far too likely.

Finally I have included some categories that are *highly* unlikely, not so much in anticipation that my book is being read by someone who fits one, but as an example of the way YOU can be more 'unique' than even an MP or member of the aristocracy with a little effort in the first place and by reading my book.

Probabilities for other countries may vary considerably depending on similarity of culture, but overall it may be assumed that a Uniqueness Factor obtained from United Kingdom data would be greater in comparison to the whole world (as we in general have more access to the majority of the categories than most people).

In many cases the data was similar to the rest of Western Europe and the USA except for some obvious anomalies; for example an American is more likely to have been to Disney World. Nor are the rates for developing countries likely to reflect those here in the UK (a Kenyan is more likely to have seen a wild leopard, but less likely to own most western consumer items).

However the things you DO abroad still count towards your Uniqueness Factor as long as you are British or live in the UK.

Secondly, you might ask, "Are all the data equal?"

As already mentioned, not all the data is of equal reliability and I so have tended to take the less precise data to the nearest factor of ten e.g. 1 in 100, 1 in 1,000, 1 in 1,000,000 and so on for ease of calculation. But in the overwhelming number of cases where good data was available I have often still rounded to one significant figure e.g. 1 in 3 or 1 in 30. (For the statistically-minded only – it was occasionally necessary to use two significant figures such as 1 in 25 or 1 in 1,500. Calculations of your Uniqueness Factor should not be unduly affected by these assumptions.)

In a shared household there may be some debate as to who actually owns something – such as the house, car or domestic appliance. While this is hardly likely to be critical

I have assumed one person can claim ownership,
NOT BOTH.
You can decide who it is ….

Also I have wrestled with the decision whether to split most of the data by gender – and have often used an average in the spirit of sex equality. However in a few highly skewed areas I have given the higher figure and noted which it related to – so if what you have done is much less likely because of your gender then add a small factor (double or triple it but no more?) – its up to you to use common sense and the advice given later.

Except where otherwise noted, I have assumed that if you were something once, or did it a long time ago – it still counts. However I have provided separate values for some occupation data. Where the original data relates primarily to numbers of currently employed, in most cases the figures provide for an estimate for no longer being current by reducing the factor by about half – i.e. 1 in 10 would become 1 in 5 and so on.

Finally a word on potentially changing data – which I have often flagged; I have endeavoured to include relatively little data which might fluctuate significantly and/or rapidly; however for some recently popular sports, hi-tech possessions and even occupations (such as call-centre worker) this has been inevitable – use your better judgement if you apply these categories.

The third question might be "Why choose exactly five things?"

Statistically if one were to multiply enough (however small) likelihoods, eventually one could achieve any Uniqueness Factor desired. This would be trivial and against the spirit of the book.

However five achievements should allow for a fair and reasonable value to be earned, providing the categories have been chosen carefully to avoid overlap (see later).

Also most of us have at least five interesting things to be proud of…

Remember it is all about
'Facts, Figures *and* Fun'.

The fourth question might be "Can you really just multiply the numbers like that?"

And the answer is NOT EXACTLY.

Inevitably there are categories that overlap: i.e. it is far more likely that you ski if you also snowboard, or if you have a Master's degree you almost certainly have a Bachelor's and so on.

So use common sense – don't combine/multiply different levels of same thing e.g. O level and A level, car driver and car owner or teacher and 'work in a school'. Use only the bigger denominator (bottom number) i.e. the lower – and therefore better – probability.

In many other cases it has been impossible for me to assess the probability of overlap, but one might still exist: e.g. are highly academic/sporting/wealthy people more (or less?) likely to travel to exotic places/ play a given sport/meet certain people etc?

I'm sorry –
you'll just have to take my best shot
and accept less accuracy.

Finally, "What if I can't find the category I want?"

I have included sections within the text for you to estimate and insert any new or additional category you wish: but first you need to know how to do this.

Without utilising the primary sources of data it is still possible to derive new values for likelihoods with a little care as long as you are prepared to accept they are likely to be less accurate than most of those found in the text.

Some examples should help: if you wish to derive a value for something which equates to a higher level of achievement than one already included simply use a 'best guess' of *how much less likely* the new achievement level is and multiply by this factor to obtain the new likelihood e.g. you are a Master Scuba Diver and know that 1 in 500 people are regular divers; you might assume that only 1 in 20 divers acquire this extra level so now the probability becomes 20 X 500 = 1 in 10,000. You must be very careful with such extrapolations. As the data is derived from regular participants in the case of most sports, it might well be that rather more actually get to this level than you thought.

If you have dived in a particularly exotic location you might like to increase your UF by 5 or so – but beware – the more exotic-seeming locations are often the most common for keen activity seekers.

Alternatively you could contact the governing body and send me the new data.

A different example might be a hobby which is simply not included; in this case look for two activities closest to it in style or format and bracket them around the new category – then choose a likelihood between the two. If you feel your achievement or activity is much less likely than any in the text, change the least likelihood by no more than 10 unless you want to overestimate your Uniqueness Factor unrealistically.

Author's Background

In the 2004 edition of the "Guinness Book of Records" I shared 1/1500th of a world record for juggling. Whilst not exactly earth shattering it put an idea in my mind: how 'unique' was I – and how could I find out?

Furthermore as a former Royal Air Force officer, commercial pilot licence holder, Master Scuba diver, 6-ball juggler, windsurfing instructor, and holder of both Bachelor's and Master's degrees, what was the probability someone else in the UK or even the world had done all those things? I began by carrying out a crude estimate and came to the conclusion that I was possibly unique because of what I had done, not just because I had been born me. And not even I had known…

But the problem was my data was unreliable.

So how could I improve it?

By finding the data for myself.

The Categories

Biological Self
Educational Qualifications
Sports
Games
World Travel
Vehicle Transport
Language & Achievements
Weird and Amazing!
Memberships
Employment & Occupations
Meeting Famous People
My Pets
House & Home
Possessions
Crime & Theft
Wealth and Income
Family Life
Health & Physical Attributes
Awards, Titles & Medals
Religion

Biological Self
Physical Self

Manual Laterality (Handedness) – now this is a tricky one to begin with – be honest with yourself

> **Pretty much left handed**: 1 in 20
> (famous lefties include: David Bowie, Rik Mayall, Phil Collins, Prince William, Lord Nelson and David Gower)
> **Bit of both (ambidextrous)**: 1 in 4
> **Right handed**: the rest of us
>
> HEIGHT – In bare feet
> **5'8" (1m 73cm) or taller**: 1 in 10 women
> **6'0" (1m 83cm) or taller**: 1 in 10 men
> **5'10" (1m 78cm) or taller** 1 in 100 women
> **6'3" (1m 91cm) or taller**: 1 in 100 men
> **5'0" (1m 53cm) or shorter**: 1 in 10 women
> **5'6" (1m 68cm) or shorter**: 1 in 10 men
> **4'10" (1m 48cm) or shorter**: 1 in 100 women
> **5'3" (1m 61cm) or shorter**: 1 in 100 men

Warning! Be very careful with these next two categories. Don't get too worked up, ok? Eye colour is famously hard to assess.

And there is so much cheating with hair colour (or contact lenses)!

EYE COLOUR

Green: 1 in 10
Hazel: 1 in 5
Blue: 1 in 4 – but more likely in the North of the UK or if you are blonde haired
Brown: 1 in 3
Heterochromia Iridium (genetically different coloured eyes): 1 in 1,000 (Jane Seymour the actress, lots of Dalmatian dogs, but NOT David Bowie – his eyes changed colour in a childhood accident)

HAIR COLOUR

Red: 1 in 25 – but 1 in 10 in Scotland or Ireland
Blonde 1 in 3 – see blue eyes above – don't use both categories together
Brunette/Black: the rest of us

BLOOD TYPE

Now this can be far more accurately assessed despite the fact that it was only discovered that blood came in different types in 1900

> **O Positive:** 1 in 3
> **O Negative:** 1 in 14
> **A Positive:** 1 in 3
> **A Negative:** 1 in 14
> **B Positive:** 1 in 12
> **B Negative:** 1 in 50
> **AB Positive:** 1 in 30
> **AB Negative:** 1 in 100
> **And of course 'Blue Blood':** see 'Titles' later

Multiple Births
One of twins: 1 in 40
One of triplets: 1 in 2,000
One of quadruplets or more : 1 in 50,000

You are over 100 years old: 1 in 6,000 – very slightly more for men than women, but not enough to worry about

You have a parent or grandparent over 100 years old: 1 in 1,500

Tongue Rolling Ability – if you cannot do this: 1 in 3 – there is some evidence that it can be learnt after all and might not be totally genetic.

Eye Dominance - Left eye: 1 in 10
This often correlates very closely to hand dominance but not always – to find your eye dominance hold up one finger and look past it into the distance (say at a wall) – you will see 'two fingers' – line up the more 'obvious' (it should be simple to choose) finger with some point in the distance and close each eye alternately – when you close the dominant eye the finger will seem to jump to the side but with only the dominant eye open the finger will remain lined up with the point.

Beard Growth: 1 in 50 (men) have a beard – This must be treated with some care – some people alternate being clean shaven with beard growth while certain cultural issues mean a beard is effectively mandatory.

Mental Self

Personality type – for this you need to have taken some kind of Personality Test (such as Myers-Briggs), many of which now use the same 16 categories often grouped into the following four main types:

> **Guardian** (SJ – Sensing Judger): 1 in 2
> **Artisan** (SP – Sensing Perceiver): 1 in 3
> **Rational** (NT- Intuitive Thinker): 1 in 10
> **Idealist** (NF – Intuitive Feeler): 1 in 10

Intelligence – there are several accepted measures – and its probably not a good idea to factor this in with your academic qualifications – but then you were smart enough to figure that out, right?

IQ (Stanford-Binet scale) – strictly speaking this is designed and accurate up to early adulthood so check which test you use – the variation is small but the Cattell and Terman indices are two of the most common others):

> **Gifted – over 130:** 1 in 30
> **Highly Gifted – over 140:** 1 in 150
> **Extremely Gifted – over 160:** 1 in 10,000
> **Profoundly Gifted – over 180:** 1 in 1,000,000!

Sexual Orientation and Gender

Gay: 1 in 12
(many great stars of screen and stage
including Oscar Wilde, Stephen Fry,
Sir Elton John, Sir Ian McKellen,
as well as Alan Turing 'code breaker
extraordinaire', Plato and Achilles)

Female: 1 in 2

Male: 1 in 2

Transsexual: 1 in 5,000

How to improve your Biological Self Uniqueness Factor

It is not generally a good idea to play 'god' with your Biological Self – mentally or physically. Sex change operations will not improve the uniqueness factor thank goodness; nor does trying to use a sharp, rapidly rotating device with your right hand while your eyes are shut or spending years using only your left hand for everything seem advisable for an increase of only ten; personality is considered by psychologists to be a fairly consistent trait (disease and brain injury notwithstanding!), and while there is some evidence that IQ can be improved the effort might be better employed in taking an exotic holiday; blood transfusions can temporarily affect blood type, but your body – if it does not reject it very painfully (type O is the Universal Donor) will soon replace it anyway! You should of course look after your parents and grandparents so they live longer but it might be quite a wait! As for eye/hair colour – enough said already!

Now if only you could clone a twin of yourself... or, alternatively, grow a beard?

Overleaf you will find the first of a number of pages in which you will find spaces to record your scores from each group of sections to make it easier to find your ultimate Uniqueness Factor.

PERSONAL LOG FOR BIOLOGICAL SELF

(to remind yourself how to complete this page look again at pages 11 and 23)

Categories	Likelihood
Manual Laterality: _____	_____
Height: _____	_____
Eye Colour:_____	_____
Hair Colour:_____	_____
Blood type:_____	_____
Personality type:_____	_____
IQ: _____	_____
Sexual orientation and Gender:_____	_____
New Categories: _____	_____
_____	_____
Estimated Likelihood	

DAVID BOWIE

Married (to Supermodel Imam –
but it doesn't count extra): 1 in 2
Paints: 1 in 10
Skis: 1 in 30
Left handed: 1 in 20
Heart bypass surgery: 1 in 100

Uniqueness Factor

................in..........................

(see how to do this in the relevant section earlier)

*And for a little further interest –
he also has two different colour eyes but due to
childhood injury not Heterochromia Iridium*

ROWAN ATKINSON

Married: 1 in 2
Higher degree (MSc): 1 in 50
Motor sports fan: 1 in 200
HGV licence holder: 1 in 30
Plays tennis: 1 in 50

Uniqueness Factor

................in..........................

*And for a little further interest –
while quite definitely nothing like 'Mr Bean' in real
life he has been known to drive and crash fast cars*

SIR PATRICK MOORE

Blue Peter Badge holder: 1 in 100
Enjoys watching cricket: 1 in 150
Plays chess: 1 in 25
Musician
(xylophone player and composer):
1 in 11
Enjoys watching Tennis and has been to
Wimbledon: 1 in 50

Uniqueness Factor

................in...........................

*And for a little further interest -
he is a Former RAF officer (World War II)*

DAVID DIMBLEBY

Has more than two (four) children: 1 in 15
Private School: 1 in 15
Oxford University (MA): 1 in 200
(NB Highest value only used)
Been to Africa: 1 in 15
Been to United States: 1 in 6

Uniqueness Factor

................in...........................

Educational Qualifications

Qualification achieved:

O levels/GCSEs at grade C or above or some NVQ:
None at all? Oops!: 1 in 3!
Fewer than 5 O levels or NVQ level equivalent:
1 in 2 (Sir Richard Branson only got 3!)
At least 5 O levels or one A level or NVQ level 2: 1 in 2

A levels –
At least 2 A levels or NVQ level 3: 1 in 3
3 or more A levels at grade A: 1 in 50

Any HE qualification (including Higher National Certificate or Diploma HNC/D or NVQ level 4):
1 in 5

Bachelor's Degree or higher (BA, BSc, LLB etc): 1 in 6

Master's Degree (MA, MSc, MB etc):
1 in 50
More specifically a coveted MBA :
1 in 200

Doctorate (PhD, DPhil, etc):
1 in 250

Graduate of one of world top 20 universities (Oxford 5th, Cambridge 6th, LSE 11th, Imperial 14th):
1 in 200
(all those MPs and spies included!)

Failed degree despite all the effort of getting in:
1 in 40
(Famous drop outs include: HG Wells - Imperial College; Bill Gates, Harvard; Woody Allen and Bruce Willis).

Public school boy:
1 in 15

Boarder:
1 in 100
('Flashman', 'Harry Potter', Jeremy Clarkson).

N.B. The trend is for academic pass rates to rise so the proportions passing this year are much higher on average than over the lifetime of the UK population in general – I have used an overall average for the country. Also those with other qualifications may have to use the nearest equivalent.

How to improve your Qualifications Uniqueness Factor

As many more people go to 'uni' these days, just getting there is no longer the crux, so try a different tack:

Drink too much and play lots of sports to reduce the chance of passing your degree! (But see also the Health and Sports sections).

But seriously, Continuing Education courses are more readily available than ever before from your local Further or Higher Education College and if the "Full Monty" (that elusive degree) is your aim, remember:

Mature applicants form 60% of all university students (large proportion of the OU and part-time courses) but the place to go has got to be the River Thames area of London where they comprise over half the full-time students of the Universities of Thames Valley and the South Bank!

And if you do drop out or haven't gone yet it's never too late to catch up – Dr Curtis Sparkes got his PhD from UMIST in 1991 at the age of 96.

PERSONAL LOG FOR QUALIFICATIONS

Categories	Likelihood
Highest Qualification Level:	
_____	_____
_____	_____
School, College or University:	
_____	_____
_____	_____
_____	_____
_____	_____
New Categories:	
_____	_____
_____	_____
Estimated Likelihood	[ ]

Sting (Gordon Sumner)

Formerly a Primary School Teacher: 1 in 100
Speaks Portuguese: 1 in 100
Had (very) Blond hair: 1 in 3
More than two (six) children: 1 in 15
Definitely gives more than £50 pa to
charity (has written a book about the
Amazon Rainforest): 1 in 20

Uniqueness Factor
................in...........................

And for a little further interest -
'Sting' is just a stage name from a striped sweater
he used to wear!

Dame Diana Rigg

Private School: 1 in 15
5' 8½" tall: 1 in 10
Enjoys reading: 1 in 2
Oxford University (Emeritus Fellow –
St Catherine's): 1 in 200
Been to (lived there actually and
speaks a little Hindi) India: 1 in 50

Uniqueness Factor
................in...........................

Sir Cliff Richard

No children: 1 in 3
Changed name (from Harry Rodger Webb): 1 in 50
Plays tennis: 1 in 50
Enjoys wine-making (owns a vineyard): 1 in 150
Gives more than £50 to charity (is a senior
member of numerous charitable organisations):
1 in 20

Uniqueness Factor

................in...........................

JODIE KIDD

Played Polo (England Women's team):
1 in 10,000
6' 1" tall: 1 in 100
Married: 1 in 2
Been to USA: 1 in 6
Blonde haired: 1 in 3

Uniqueness Factor

................in...........................

Outdoor Sports: Team

Most data in the sports, hobbies & games sections are for 'regular participants' unless specifically stated.

If you participate only 'occasionally' you may need to change the *Uniqueness Factor by half so for example 1 in 20 would score 1 in 10 and so on.

If you are a qualified coach/instructor/referee/umpire increase the unlikelihood factor by 10 i.e. 1 in 3 becomes 1 in 30!! This also applies to all later sports and games sections!

Of course if you happen to be so good you are nationally ranked or in a professional league (the above figures already allow for the 'weekend sportsman') you probably know your position anyway and don't need my help.

However if your sport, game or hobby doesn't appear you can be pretty sure it either has a lower probability than most of those that do OR it is so popular that it is done by more than 50% of people.

Estimating a Uniqueness Factor for such a case can be done as described earlier in the Introduction.

First your general 'Sportiness' level –

Playing any competitive sport:
only 1 in 3 adults play at all.

Being a member of any type of sports club:
1 in 5

The Sports

Association Football (soccer): 1 in 20
(1 in 10 men)
Bowls: 1 in 75
Cricket: 1 in 150
**Member of the Primary Club charity
(bowled out for a duck first ball!):**
1 in 4,000
Field Hockey: 1 in 300
Ice Hockey: 1 in 2,000
Netball: 1 in 300 (women)
Rugby League: 1 in 2,000
Rugby Union: 1 in 250

Outdoor Sports: Individual

N.B. Most data are for 'regular participants'. If you participate 'occasionally' typically the factor is half as big so 1 in 20 would be 1 in 10 or so. And if you are a coach/instructor you may increase any given factor by times 10

A member of any type of sports club:
1 in 5

Archery (toxophily): 1 in 2,500
Badminton: 1 in 50
Bowls (includes indoors): 1 in 75
Canoeing/Kayaking: 1 in 50

Caving: 1 in 1,000
Climbing/Mountaineering: 1 in 150
Croquet: 1 in 5,000
Cycling: 1 in 10
Fishing: 1 in 15
Gliding: 1 in 1,000 (1 in 50,000 women)

Golf: 1 in 20 overall (1 in 10 men)
  With better than 10 handicap: 1 in 2,000
  (ie 1 in 100 golfers)
  Achieved a 'Hole in One' in lifetime:
  1 in 800 (ie 1 in 40 golfers)

Horse Riding: 1 in 100 overall (1 in 50 women)
  Show Jumping: 1 in 200
  Three Day Eventing: 1 in 1,000

Motor Sports: 1 in 200
Motor Cycling: 1 in 500

Parachuting/skydiving: 1 in 100 ever done it
(1 in 10,000 still current)
Pilot: 1 in 1,000
Airline/commercial licence holder: 1 in 2,000
(1 in 25,000 women!)
Private licence holder only: 1 in 2,500
(1 in 20,000 women)
Helicopter: 1 in 10,000 (1 in 100,000 women!)
Balloon: 1 in 60,000
Paramotoring: 1 in 5,000
Polo: 1 in 10,000

Rollerblading: 1 in 500
(Robbie Williams)

Running: 1 in 20
  Athletics/Track and Field: 1 in 500
  Half marathon: 1 in 100
  Full Marathon: 1 in 200

Sailing
  Dinghy: 1 in 50
  Yachting: 1 in 100
Shooting (all disciplines): 1 in 125
  Clay pigeon: 1 in 100
  Full bore: 1 in 500
  Small bore: 1 in 500
  Crossbow: 1 in 500,000
Snow (winter) sports
  All: 1 in 20
  Downhill Skiing: 1 in 30
  Snowboarding: 1 in 125
  Cross country skiing: 1 in 2,500

Tennis: 1 in 50

Watersports
  Water Skiing: 1 in 100 – 1 in 75 (men),
  1 in 150 (women). Interestingly only 10%
  are thought to be potential participants – so
  that says a lot about our national fitness!
  Windsurfing: 1 in 100
  Surfing: 1 in 500
  Kitesurfing/sailing: 1 in 3,000
  Rowing: 1 in 100
  Scuba Diving: 1 in 500

Indoor Sports

N.B. Most data are for regular participants. If you participate occasionally typically the factor is half as big so 1 in 20 would be 1 in 10 or so.

And if you are a coach/instructor you may increase any given factor by times 10.

Member of any type of Sports Club: 1 in 5

Basketball: 1 in 150
Martial Arts (all): 1 in 100
Judo: 1 in 500 (Kate Howey MP)
Karate: 1 in 500
Kung Fu: 1 in 1,000
– Black belt in any of above: 1 in 10,000
Boxing: 1 in 500
Wrestling: 1 in 300

Ice Skating: 1 in 100
Fencing: 1 in 1,000
Gymnastics: 1 in 300 (but much higher for kids!)
Squash: 1 in 75
Swimming: 1 in 7
– not exactly indoor but if you've swum the English Channel: 1 in 100,000 ever!

Table tennis: 1 in 75
Ten Pin Bowling: 1 in 25
Volleyball: 1 in 500
Weight training: 1 in 15
Weightlifting: 1 in 75

Phil Collins

Left-handed: 1 in 20
5' 6" tall: 1 in 10
Has more than two (five) children: 1 in 15
Is an 'expat' (lives in Switzerland): 1 in 25
Also plays the piano: 1 in 50

Uniqueness Factor

................in...........................

*And for a little further interest –
has a facial scar from a car crash*

Lisa Stansfield

Married (to music co-writer): 1 in 2
Does crosswords: 1 in 20
Paints: 1 in 10
Cookery fan: 1 in 4
Been to Japan : 1 in 200

Uniqueness Factor

................in...........................

Anne Robinson

Red hair: 1 in 25
Private (Convent) School: 1 in 15
Had face-lift: 1 in 50
Loves her dogs: 1 in 6
Likes cooking: 1 in 4

Uniqueness Factor

................in...........................

*And for a little further interest -
has been President or Vice-President of both
a cricket and tennis club*

Sue Lawley

Has two Children: 1 in 3
BA degree: 1 in 6
- And in Modern Languages: 1 in 100
Skis: 1 in 30
Plays Bridge: 1 in 20

Uniqueness Factor

................in...........................

How to improve your Sports Uniqueness Factor

Considering the apparently declining participation in team sports and club memberships (we are well behind the French, Germans and Dutch in this respect) you can justifiably be proud of any achievement in these sections. But a good run round on a fog shrouded soggy mud patch might just be a little too much for some – and that's just cricket...

If you are feeling truly enthusiastic try your local sports ground or centre or contact 'Sport UK' for guidance.

The recent tendency towards more individual sporting activities allows for a very wide choice – a word of warning – these are often associated with varying degrees of danger either to you or others so check with the relevant National Governing Body to make sure you have qualified instruction. The National Sports Centres are a good start. The Royal Yachting Association (RYA), Ski Club of Great Britain SCGB), British Waterski Federation (BWSF), British Canoe Union (BCU), Aircraft Owners and Pilots Association (AOPA UK), British Gliding Association (BGA), National Rifle Associations (NRA/ NRSA) or the Grand National Archery Society (GNAS) – make sure to buy green clothes and move to Sherwood Forest – amongst others will give excellent advice.

But don't be put off, a little risk adds to the adrenalin rush!

Martial Arts score highly and given the present state of personal crime might be a very good bet! Don't underestimate the level of commitment necessary to achieve a decent standard however – and you might need to stock up on pain-killers and bandages…

Alternatively just run a Marathon dressed in the weirdest clothes while also juggling or playing a musical instrument and calculate your own UF.

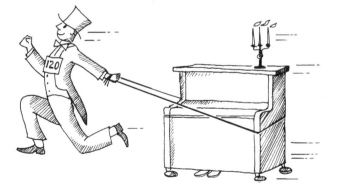

PERSONAL LOG FOR SPORTS

Categories	Likelihood
Outdoor Sports– Team Sports:	
_____	_____
_____	_____
Individual Sports:	
_____	_____
_____	_____
Indoor Sports –	
_____	_____
_____	_____
New Categories:	
_____	_____
Estimated Likelihood	

Games

Of course there are a lot more games than these –
too many in fact to list – but this should give you an
idea of the more established ones. Some others can
be found in Hobbies.

Cards –
Poker: 1 in 10
Contract Bridge: 1 in 20

Chess –
Play for fun: 1 in 25
Have British Chess Federation (BCF)
grading: 1 in 4,000
Grand/International - Master level:
men 1 in 100,000
women – you are 1 in 1,000,000 already!

Darts: 1 in 20

Juggling –
Three balls (for at least ten throws):
1 in 50
Five or more balls juggled: 1 in 500

Poker (internet): 1 in 15

Snooker/Pool/Billiards: 1 in 6 (men)

Hobbies

Astronomy: 1 in 1,500
Bee Keeping (Apiarism): 1 in 2,500
    (Pam Ayres and Mick Jagger)
Bell Ringing (Campanology): 1 in 1,000
Bingo: 1 in 10
Bird Watching (Twitching or Birding):
1 in 20
    (Bill Oddie, Harold 'Dickie' Bird,
    Freddie Trueman)
Crossword solving:
    Cryptic: 1 in 20
    General Knowledge: 1 in 15
Cookery: 1 in 4
Collecting Coins (numismatics): 1 in 50
Collecting Stamps (philately): 1 in 25
Collecting Antiques: 1 in 10
Collecting Comics: 1 in 50
    (mostly men – but lots more children)
Dowsing (water divining): 1 in 25,000
DIY: 1 in 7
Fossil Hunting: 1 in 500
Gardening/plant growing: 1 in 2
Keep Fit/Yoga: 1 in 10 overall
    (1 in 6 women)
Kite flying; 1 in 30
Knitting/dressmaking/needlework: 1 in 4
Magic: 1 in 100
Model Aircraft –
    Flying: 1 in 1,000
    Making: 1 in 100

National Lottery:
1 in 2 every week
1 in 5 never played
Naturism: 1 in 50
Pub Quizzes: 1 in 30
Train Spotting: 1 in 300
Plane Spotting: 1 in 500
Sudoku: 1 in 10
    (Carol Vorderman - very trendy at
    present!)
Video Games: 1 in 5
Walking: 1 in 3
– for Charity: 1 in 60
Wine-making: 1 in 150
War games: 1 in 500
Woodworking: 1 in 50

Jonny Wilkinson

Private School: 1 in 15
Single: 1 in 3
Blue Peter Badge: 1 in 100
Guitarist: 1 in 50
Left-handed (Left-footed!): 1 in 20

Uniqueness Factor

................in..........................

*And for a little further interest -
has been to Australia and was admitted to
Hospital for a Sports related Shoulder Injury*

Kelly Holmes

Single: 1 in 3
Blue Peter Badge: 1 in 100
Nurse: 1 in 50
Armed Forces NCO (Army): 1 in 60
Has been South of the Equator:
1 in 15

Uniqueness Factor

................in..........................

Artistic and Leisure Activities

You have to be honest again here – it really only counts if you have done it recently and/or regularly, except in the case of playing a musical instrument – as long as you have learned it, it still counts.

Acting: 1 in 50
Caravanning: 1 in 25
Dancing: 1 in 10
Painting: 1 in 10
Photography: 1 in 15
Reading: 1 in 2

Singing/playing musical instrument:
1 in 11
In a band/group: 1 in 20
Choral Society: 1 in 15
Piano: 1 in 30
Guitar: 1 in 50
Violin: 1 in 150
Brass: 1 in 50
Drums: (look, everyone thinks they can but...): 1 in 40

And just for the 'professionals'! –

Associated Boards of the Royal Schools of Music Grades:
    Passed anything at Grade 8
    (the highest): 1 in 200
    Diploma level: 1 in 3,000

Writing (stories or poems): 1 in 25

Events attended on a regular basis: – either once a month in the season or at least 6 times a year

    Live sports: 1 in 5
    Association Football: 1 in 100
    Rugby Union: 1 in 500
    Cricket: 1 in 150

    Theatre (play/drama): 1 in 4
    Art gallery: 1 in 4
    Classical (or jazz) Music: 1 in 7
    Opera: 1 in 14
    Ballet: 1 in 14
    Dance show: 1 in 20
    Circus/carnival: 1 in 5
    Rock concert: 1 in 5

Don't usually go to Cinema: 1 in 3(!)
Don't read a daily newspaper: 1 in 3

Watch more than 7 hours of TV per day: 1 in 10

Don't watch any TV at least one day per week: 1 in 10

And if you don't watch TV, listen to the radio or play music you are 1 in 100 at least!

Slightly bigger events you might have been to perhaps as a 'once in a lifetime' occasion:

British Lions rugby tour of New Zealand in 2005: 1 in 3,000

The Ashes Tests in 2005: 1 in 500

Up the London Eye (UK's most popular private tourist attraction): 1 in 25

Glastonbury: 1 in 300
Edinburgh Festival: 1 in 100

Wembley (FA Cup finals and full internationals only): 1 in 12

Twickenham (full internationals only): 1 in 30

Lord's (full internationals only): 1 in 40

Wimbledon: 1 in 50

How to improve your Games, Hobbies, Artistic and Leisure Activities Uniqueness Factor

We Brits do appear to be quite a nation of games enthusiasts and hobbyists (which perhaps explains our reluctance to go outside and get muddy as mentioned!), so to score highly in this section you have to do pretty unusual things – what a surprise! Spotting and hoarding things definitely get the uniqueness factor up – whether it's worth the effect on the social life is another matter! Of course you could always do them in the buff, thus improving (?) your chance of meeting people... (unless you choose Bell Ringing and pull the wrong thing!). Oh, and definitely keep the kit on for Bee Keeping!

Of course IF you actually win 'big' on the Lottery you get to have the last laugh – though you do have a better chance of being struck by lightning...

For those out of the ordinary activities to make life more interesting you might wish to try contacting such organizing bodies as the British Bee Keeping Association (BBKA), British Chess federation (BCF), British Astronomical Society (BAS), The Magic Circle or even the Central Council of Church Bell Ringers.

Or if you are up to the challenge, learn that musical instrument you always wanted to play – to the Royal Schools of Music standard of course.

But to be perfectly honest, from time to time you simply need to get out a lot more – literally! Live stuff is the way to go, whether it's sport or a show – better still go to another country at the same time! Just don't think playing the internet will in any way prepare you for the Las Vegas poker challenge!

Which brings us nicely onto World Travel in just a moment...

PERSONAL LOG FOR GAMES, HOBBIES, ARTISTIC & LEISURE ACTIVITIES

Categories	Likelihood
Hobbies:	
Games:	
Artistic Activities:	
Leisure Activities:	
New Categories:	
Estimated Likelihood	

World Travel

Do not have a passport (just the same proportion of Americans DO have one!): 1 in 5

Have taken 5 or more holidays overseas in the last year: 1 in 40

Have ever been to USA/Canada: 1 in 6
  Disneyland/World: 1 in 20
  Las Vegas: 1 in 40
  Hawai'i: 1 in 200
  Niagara Falls: 1 in 100
  Yellowstone Park: 1 in 100

Former USSR/Russia: 1 in 250
Australasia: 1 in 40
India: 1 in 50
  And have seen a tiger in the wild:
  1 in 5,000
Japan: 1 in 200
China (including Hong Kong): 1 in 200
  Mainland: 1 in 2,000

Africa: 1 in 15
  Have seen a leopard in the wild: 1 in 5,000 (and the ones they bait with goats are cheating really!)
  Seen a wild lion: 1 in 50
  Seen a wild elephant: 1 in 75
  Went gorilla trekking (wild ones actually seen): 1 in 100,000

Seen a wild rhino: 1 in 150

Famous sites visited –
Macchu Picchu: 1 in 500
Petra (Jordan): 1 in 500
(it's so much better than it looks in
the Indiana Jones movie)
The Great Pyramids: 1 in 25

Modes of transport used –
Aircraft: more than 1 in 2
Flown first class: 1 in 100
Ship: 1 in 20
Train –
First class: 1 in 10
Orient Express in Europe: 1 in 1,000

And in order from North to South! –
Visited North Pole/arctic icecap: 1 in 5,000
Crossed (while airborne doesn't count!)
Arctic Circle (66 deg 32 min N): 1 in 500
Saw Aurora Borealis
(Actually knowing that is the correct name
for the Northern Lights scores pretty highly
itself: 1 in 5!): 1 in 30
Saw Aurora Australis (Southern Lights):
1 in 500
Crossed equator: 1 in 15
Crossed dateline: 1 in 2,000 while in the air
but 1 in 20,000 while on 'terra firma'.
Crossed the Antarctic Circle
(66 deg 32 min S): 1 in 15,000
Visited South Pole/Antarctica: 1 in 25,000

Been in a Tropical Rainforest: 1 in 150

Are or have been an expatriate
(the largest proportion is pensioners living
in Australia!): 1 in 25

Stayed in a five star hotel: 1 in 200

Climbed –
    Mt Everest: 1 in 300,000
    Kilimanjaro: 1 in 2,500
    The Rockies (even by car): 1 in 25

And a few others which could happen
all over the world –
    Swum with dolphins: 1 in 250
    Swum with sharks: 1 in 400

    But just so we don't leave out
    'home sweet home' –

Have been to Stonehenge: 1 in 10
Have been to the Dome: 1 in 30

Have experienced a tornado (winds
typically 70 to 100mph):
    Only saw it: 1 in 500
    Were affected by it: 1 in 5,000

Have felt an earthquake measuring greater
than 5 on the Richter Scale
(very few in the UK in recorded history):
1 in 5,000

How to improve your World Travel Uniqueness Factor

First get that old passport renewed just in case – with all the new rules on 'biometric' data and needing six months or more remaining on the thing you might find the best places won't let you in – or worse – not let you out again!

You might also need vaccinations (unless your phobia is needles), new clothes – the safari suit went out a loooong time ago – and a good guidebook.

Now that's all fixed don't take the easy way – baited wild animals (a goat carcass hanging in a tree just waiting for a leopard) really is cheating and while you might not get to see what you want the thrill of a genuine safari or primate trek will be fascinating. The Wildlife Trust/Protection Society of India will help with tigers; there is so much choice in the African continent so all I can say is choose carefully; shark swimming/viewing especially from a cage is not for the faint hearted and might result in scoring an unwanted (are there any others?) hospital admission pretty much ruining that trip down south. Perhaps a little safer – but not to be taken lightly – are dolphins. Finally if all you want to do is watch whales from a boat you won't score anything but the Pacific North West of North America is awesome.

Best places to see/find things

The Arctic Circle and Aurora Borealis might be combined – weather permitting – with a visit to Finland or Iceland (but once there you must take a trip to Grimsey Island – and only in summer). Sweden, Canada (especially Yellowknife) and of course Siberia offer even more options depending on your adventurousness.

'Dorothyland' or 'Tornado Alley' in the US Midwest offers a much better(?) chance of experiencing a twister than pretty well anywhere else in the world, whilst nearer to home try the south west of England for the best chance of encountering one of the 30 or so tornadoes that appear in Britain each year, or North Wales for the much rarer occurrence of an earthquake.

For the beach bound, the world's first 'six star' hotel sets the standards for all the rest. The Burj Al Arab forms the 'Wave' half of the 'Wave & Sail' pair of hotels on the Jumeirah beach coast of Dubai, United Arab Emirates: maybe you could brush up on a foreign language at the same time?

Vehicle Transport

Do *not* hold any Driving Licence: 1 in 3

Hold licence for:
   PSV: 1 in 80
   LGV (old HGV): 1 in 30
   Motorcycle: 1 in 25

Have a personalised number plate:
– that actually means something, not simply letters that look odd: 1 in 1,000
– that just looks 'different': 1 in 10
'Talk' to your car: 1 in 2
Worry about your car's "feelings": 1 in 5
Have a pet name for your car: 1 in 5
(women)
Have a satellite navigation system installed: 1 in 10 motorists - but can you use it properly...?

Modes of Transport used

Owner of offshore class boat: 1 in 300
Owner of plane: 1 in 3,000
Pilot's licence holder: 1 in 1,000
Train Driver: 1 in 1,500

Type of car owned

Don't own a car!: 1 in 4
Van/commercial vehicle: 1 in 7
SUV: 1 in 30
Motorcycle: 1 in 40
3 or more cars: 1 in 20
Diesel car: 1 in 6
LPG car: 1 in 30,000
Electric vehicle: 1 in 10,000
'Old' car (pre '85): 1 in 150
Car older than you: 1 in 300
Vintage (pre 1930) sports car: 1 in 3,000
Traction (steam) engine: 1 in 15,000
Caravan: 1 in 25

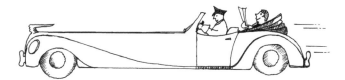

How to improve your Vehicle Transport Uniqueness Factor

Just get out of the rut of driving a boring saloon. Buy that old sports car or motorcycle you've always wanted or take an LGV test (too literal a following of the advice in this book might occasionally result in you joining the ranks of the recently but not currently married – see Family Life!).

The author will accept no responsibility for such fateful decisions!

For those less constrained by common sense or responsibility cut yourself free from those surly bonds and learn to fly or sail – but remember 'a boat is just a hole in the water into which you throw money' and as for a 'plane' – the phrase 'burning money' comes to mind…

PERSONAL LOG FOR WORLD TRAVEL & VEHICLE TRANSPORT

Categories	Likelihood
Countries or Places visited:	
Sights Seen:	
Methods of Transport Used:	
Personal Vehicles:	
Other:	
New Categories:	
Estimated Likelihood	

Boris Johnson

Paints: 1 in 10
Skis: 1 in 30
Writes poetry: 1 in 25
Has blond hair: 1 in 3
Loves to cycle!: 1 in 10

Uniqueness Factor
................in...........................

*And for a little further interest –
he was admitted to hospital following a cycling
collision with a pedestrian thus contributing highly
to the other chap's UF!*

Jo(hanne) Whiley

Snowboards: 1 in 125
Swims: 1 in 7
Windsurfs: 1 in 100
Plays volleyball: 1 in 500
Has more than two children: 1 in 15

Uniqueness Factor

................in...........................

*And for a little further interest -
likes to go barefoot on TV*

Hugh Grant

Has a criminal record (procured a prostitute):
1 in 50
BA degree: 1 in 6
Single: 1 in 3
Football fan (Fulham): 1 in 100
Owns a second (actually seventeen!) home:
1 in 200

Uniqueness Factor

................in...........................

Sir Richard Branson

Achieved fewer than 5 O levels
(Due in part to dyslexia): 1 in 2
Plays tennis: 1 in 50
Skis: 1 in 30
Balloons (holds world record for Atlantic and
Pacific crossings): 1 in 500
Member of Mile High Club: 1 in 1,000

Uniqueness Factor
................in...........................

Sir Mick Jagger

Has more than two (seven) children: 1 in 15
Went to university (London School of Economics)
but did not finish: 1 in 40
Has ballooned over Manhattan: 1 in 500
Lived as an expatriate (in France): 1 in 25
Likes beekeeping: 1 in 2,500

Uniqueness Factor

................in...........................

Rod Stewart

Has more than two (five) children: 1 in 15
Football mad
(was on the books of Brentford FC): 1 in 100
Blond haired: 1 in 3
Has suffered from (thyroid) cancer: 1 in 50
Wears spectacles
(was top of a sexiest wearers poll in 2004):
1 in 2

Uniqueness Factor

................in...........................

Language

Languages are not a strong point here in Britain – despite there being around seven thousand languages on the planet – any attempt to master another one earns respect, especially after being subjected to our school system! However the government's new "Language Ladder" is a great idea to begin with and with the expansion of the EU, all the more valuable.

Speak any language 'conversationally' other than English: 1 in 3

And in order of 'how commonly spoken' –
    French: 1 in 5
    German: 1 in 15
    Spanish: 1 in 30
    Italian: 1 in 40
    Other European: 1 in 100

Speak any two foreign languages' conversationally:
1 in 20

"Can I have a beer?" in five languages:
1 in 25!
(shouting doesn't count!)

Actually having a qualification at A level or higher:
1 in 100

Now here are a few ways to improve that uniqueness factor – although the 'coolness' factor might take a bit of a dive...

Klingon: 1 in a 1,000,000 – If that many!
Elvish: 1 in a 1,000,000 – ditto!
Esperanto: 1 in 1,000
Lojban: 1 in 5,000,000 – talk to the machines for when they take over the earth!
Choctaw: only 1 in 30,000 Native Americans do so. If you are British and can speak it – 1 in a 1,000,000

But if the earlier ones are too much for now, stick to some slightly easier targets:
Ancient Greek: 1 in 1,000
Latin: 1 in 500
Chinese (Mandarin or Cantonese): 1 in 250
Japanese: 1 in 250
Arabic: 1 in 100
Russian: 1 in 100
Cornish: 1 in 5,000
Welsh: 1 in 100
Scots Gaelic: 1 in 500
Sign language: 1 in 5,000 if you are not hearing impaired (1 in 500 if you are).
Urdu/Hindi/Punjabi: Approximately 1 in 25 people speak these as a first language rather than a second one so it is very hard to estimate how many are genuine second language speakers in the UK – perhaps 1 in 1,000

How to improve your Language Uniqueness Factor

Start with Sign Language or Greek and move up to Klingon or Elvish! (Lots of internet sites have beginner's advice – you have been warned!).

Try the National Centre for Language Training (CILT) or your local FE/HE college prospectus to enliven those TV nights just for a start, but how about an exotic holiday with a new language combined – total immersion into a culture has to be the way to go for the committed.

Contact the British or American Sign Language organisations and learn a valuable and different linguistic skill.

You might even just help the kids with their homework and realise how much/little you already knew…

Achievements

Actually have been named in the
Guinness Book of World Records: 1 in 5,000
Have been in the "GBWR" as part of a group
record: 1 in 500

Been a film/TV extra (non-professionally):
1 in 500
Aircraft Pilot (see sports)
Been arrested – not one to try for honestly!
(See Crime)
Been ballooning: 1 in 500
Been down a coal mine: 1 in 150
Been in a police line-up: 1 in 50
Been in a TV audience: 1 in 250
Been on a jury: 1 in 4 (MPs, Armed/Police
Forces, insane and criminals can't be – just
checking!)
Been on Reality TV show: 1 in 750
Been on TV quiz/game show: 1 in 500
Been seen on TV: 1 in 500
Been heard on radio: 1 in 200
Blue Peter Badge holder: 1 in 100
Boarded the BA London Eye: 1 in 30
Bought this Book: 1 in 'insert self-calculation'
based on latest Best-seller lists data! [Hopeful
Author!]
Bungee jumped: 1 in 50

Changed name –
> **By Deed Poll:** 1 in 5,000 (not all name changes are done this way and of course this does not include marriage!).
> **By choice:** 1 in 50

Climbed mountains: – see World Travel & Transport
Cryptic Prize Crossword winner –
National newspapers papers only: 1 in 5,000
Delivered a baby: 1 in 400
Donated blood: 1 in 40
Donated Egg – only women!
> (Within last year): 1 in 15,000

Donated Sperm – only men!
> (Within last year): 1 in 60,000

Flown in a glider: 1 in 200
Flown in a light aircraft/helicopter: 1 in 250
Had a poem, photograph or magazine article published (unless you work for the newspaper) **in a national newspaper**: 1 in 700
> **Local newspaper:** 1 in 300

Had a letter published in:
> **Local newspaper:** 1 in 100
> **National newspaper:** 1 in 250

Lottery Jackpot winners 1 in 30,000

Patented something –
> **Applied for a patent:** 1 in 500
> **Were granted one:** 1 in 5,000

Have sung karaoke: 1 in 5
(of whom 1 in 10 were not brave enough
to have sung it solo!)

Saved someone's life (in last year – excluding medics): 1 in 5,000
Seen a meteor shower: 1 in 10
Seen a comet (most probably Hale-Bopp or Halley's): 1 in 10
Seen a planet through a telescope (binoculars don't count – if you don't believe me – try it!): 1 in 2,500
Seen a total solar eclipse: 1 in 5,000
– and if you do get to the real thing, you'll know why I haven't included data on a partial eclipse)
Seen a space shuttle launch –
From the official launch viewing area in Florida: 1 in 100,000
From the nearest road 2 miles away: 1 in 5,000
Sold a painting: 1 in 100

Used the internet:
1 in 2 and soon to be more than this and hence trivial

Voted in last (2005) European Elections: 1 in 3
Did not vote in last (2005) General Elections: 1 in 3
Voted Conservative: 1 in 5 (NB of all electorate)
Voted Labour: 1 in 5
Voted Liberal Democrat: 1 in 8
Voted Other party: 1 in 15

Don't normally vote in any elections at all:
1 in 3

Volunteer regularly for charity work: 1 in 15

Have written a published book: 1in 500

Have been 'weightless': 1 in 1 (we all have –
but see "How to Improve your UF …")
Are a World War One survivor: At the time of
writing probably only 1 in 40,000,000
Are a World War II Survivor: 1 in 500
Made a "Who's Who" appearance: 1 in 2,000
– do you really need this book!?

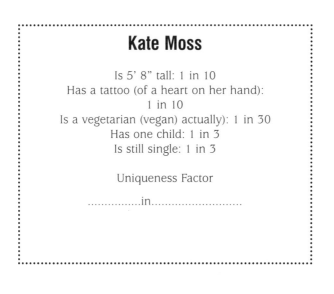

Kate Moss

Is 5' 8" tall: 1 in 10
Has a tattoo (of a heart on her hand):
1 in 10
Is a vegetarian (vegan) actually): 1 in 30
Has one child: 1 in 3
Is still single: 1 in 3

Uniqueness Factor

…………….in………………………

How to improve your Achievements Uniqueness Factor

The opportunities for improvement in this section are almost infinite – just start at the top of the page and work your way down!

Here are just a few suggestions:

The best approach to be included in the GBWR might be as part of a mass group record such as the 'greatest number of people juggling simultaneously' (yours truly was at the Edinburgh European Juggling Convention for that one!).

A balloon safari in South Africa – with a visit to the world's deepest mine – might break the bank but what a vacation to talk about back home!

Police line-ups are being replaced by video/virtual line-ups so this will become even less common as time goes by – so don't hold your breath and go for it.

If you don't want to start as a stage hand, get 'extras' work and hope for that big break in show business while waiting tables or flipping burgers. There are increasing numbers of opportunities (and applicants) for the crop of 'reality shows' in vogue – you might even be a 'celebrity' yourself.

But many people forget how much fun just being

in an audience can be – most shows have simple application procedures and the result does not involve future embarrassment and ridicule – at least not for you.

Although there is no guarantee that you will 'save someone's life' a First Aid course (contact the Red Cross, St John's Ambulance or Royal Life Saving Society) could be a more worthwhile target – this can also be combined with an activity-instructor training course to make you a Rescue Diver or Mountain Leader.

Try to invent something, but be careful to ask The Patent Office for advice and don't expect the process to be cheap.

Look up at the night sky from time to time – safely of course – or better still find a place unspoiled by light pollution and just enjoy what our ancestors would have seen with far more regularity and awe. Some of the best meteor showers are to be found in the constellations of Orion, Taurus and Leo (from mid August to November). Comets need rather more patience – you might even find yourself taking up astronomy as a hobby.

Oh, to return to the 'weightlessness' issue. A common and misguided belief is that the only way to be weightless is to hop aboard the NASA 'vomit comet' as used for astronaut training or to actually get launched into space. There is another way, but dying in a falling lift does not come with my recommendation. No, just jump up off the ground and for a spilt second you are just as weightless as in the two previous examples.

Weird and Amazing!

**Travelled supersonic
(at the speed of sound):** 1 in 500
most likely in Concorde but possibly in a
fast fighter jet – even luckier!

**Logged on to the seti@home
(Search for extra terrestrial life)
programme as amateur assistant:**
1 in 300

Seen a ghost: 1 in 3

Seen a 'big cat' wild in the UK: 1 in 2,000
(like the Beast of Bodmin or the Sydenham
Puma)

Seen a UFO (Unidentified Flying Object):
1 in 50
**And actually reported it officially to the
Ministry of Defence:** 1 in 1,000

Been hit by lightning:
1 in 20,000

**Mile High Club
(had sex above a mile high!):** 1 in 1,000
(kind of depends on how you define sex!)
**Mile High Club while on the ground
but higher than 5280 ft:** 1 in 200

(but strictly speaking it should still be while flying though you could be prosecuted too!)
Had sex while actually flying the aircraft:
1 in WOW!

Naturism practitioner: 1 in 50
**Consider yourself a transvestite
(cross dresser):** 1 in 100 (men)

Practising dowser (water diviner/witch):
1 in 25,000
Human guinea pig: 1 in 5,000
Inhaled helium gas: 1 in 10
Squeeze toothpaste tube from the bottom:
1 in 4

Use Internet Dating Agency: 1 in 10

Live(d) aboard a boat: 1 in 400

Life saved by lifeboat: 1 in 100,000
within last year or 1 in 2,000 over lifetime

Been in a cult: 1 in 30

Attended a Sci-Fi convention: 1 in 500
(mostly men!)

Seen Rocky Horror Picture show live: 1 in 500

Have a tattoo/piercing: 1 in 10 (illegal in Oklahoma)

Unfit to serve in the military (16 to 49 years old only): 1 in 6

Don't wear predominantly dark clothing for work: 1 in 10! (men only...)

Have never sewn a button on: 1 in 10

Have never been stung by an insect (don't count a 'mossie' bite): 1 in 5

Have never slept in a tent: 1 in 5

Have never lit a firework: 1 in 10

Have never changed a car wheel/tyre: 1 in 3

Have never changed a spark plug: 1 in 3

Have never ridden a donkey: 1 in 5

Have ever fainted: 1 in 5

Have taken part in a séance or used a 'Ouija' board:
1 in 5

Use car lights in daytime when it is raining:
1 in 15

How to improve your Weird & Amazing Uniqueness Factor

Move to Yorkshire – York is one of the most haunted places in the British Isles and Ryedale has one of the more 'commonly sighted' Big Cats! (Also you might want to try Bodmin or Exmoor).

Move to the USA – the most UFO friendly country in the world – where 1 in 15 people claim to have seen one!

Log onto seti@home.ssl.berkeley.edu to be a volunteer 'alien tracker'.

Move onto a boat without proper RYA training and get rescued – double score!

Take a holiday somewhere high up and hope to get lucky.

Or even campaign for the return of Concorde!

Get a Rocky Horror Show tattoo and join the cult of regulars who dress up at the show – triple score! (but make sure the tattoo is done while you are relatively sober and by a 'professional').

Contact your local research hospital and volunteer for clinical trials – just don't expect to make a fortune – and read the contract very carefully.

Finally don't play golf in the rain in case you want to qualify for a 'Darwin Award' – which will certainly exclude you from ever using this book again.

PERSONAL LOG FOR LANGUAGE, ACHIEVEMENTS, WEIRD & AMAZING

Categories	Likelihood
Languages Spoken/Level:	
	_____
Personal Achievements:	
	_____
	_____
Weird & Amazing Stuff Done:	
	_____
	_____
Other:	
	_____
New Categories:	
	_____
	_____
Estimated Likelihood	

Tony Blair

More than two (four) Children: 1 in 15
Masters degree (Oxford): 1 in 200
Lawyer: 1 in 2,000
Lives in a terraced house: 1 in 4
Book published: 1 in 500

Uniqueness Factor

................in...........................

Opik Lembit

BA degree: 1 in 6
Windsurfs: 1 in 100
Flies private aircraft: 1 in 1,000
Rides a Motorcycle: 1 in 25
Into Astronomy: 1 in 1,500

Uniqueness Factor

................in...........................

*And for your interest -
he is married to a 'Weathergirl'.*

Memberships

[In many other cases it is possible to estimate from known 'occupations' as e.g. most doctors are also members of the BMC, teachers all join the General Teaching Council, etc]

Freemasons: 1 in 100

Round Table: 1 in 5,000
Lions: 1 in 2,500
Rotary: 1 in 3,000

The "Primary Club" charity (bowled out for a duck in cricket first ball!): 1 in 4,000

Membership of any London Gentleman's' Club – think yourselves lucky! : 1 in 5,000
   Such as: **Athenaeum, Boodles, Blacks, Carlton, East India, Garrick, Reform, The RAC:** the actual London Club was formed 1897

The "Magic Circle": 1 in 15,000 men
(1 in 150,000 women)

Royal Automobile Club: 1 in 7
(this is the roadside one NOT the elite Royal Automobile Club itself!)

Automobile Association: 1 in 3
And for either of the last two you had a 1 in 15 chance of needing them in the last year!

Royal Yachting Association: 1 in 500

Royal National Lifeboat Institute: 1 in 150
Very likely to have these two in combination
– so don't multiply!

Womens' Royal Voluntary Service: 1 in 300

Womens' Institute: 1 in 150

National Trust: 1 in 20 members
(1 in 1000 volunteers)

Institute of Advanced Motorists: 1 in 500

Any Trade Union: 1 in 4
Equity: 1 in 1,000
Amicus: 1 in 40
UNISON: 1 in 40
NUT: 1 in 250
TGWU: 1 in 50

Julie Walters

HE certificate: 1 in 5
Teacher: 1 in 100
Likes reading: 1 in 2
Married: 1 in 2
5' 8" tall: in 10

Uniqueness Factor

.................in...........................

Carol Vorderman

Single: 1 in 3
Two children: 1 in 3
IQ of 167: 1 in 10,000
Cambridge University (MA degree):
1 in 200
Is a keen exponent of the art of Sudoku:
1 in 10

Uniqueness Factor

.................in...........................

Jeremy Clarkson

Married: 1 in 2
6' 4" tall; 1 in 100
Has written a book: 1 in 500
Private School: 1 in 15
Into motor sports: 1 in 200

Uniqueness Factor

................in...........................

JK Rowling

Married: 1 in 2
Likes rock music (The Smiths): 1 in 5
BA degree: 1 in 6
Was a teacher: 1 in 100
Lived as an expatriate
(in Portugal while writing first
'Harry Potter' book): 1 in 25

Uniqueness Factor

................in...........................

Employment

*"Employment statistics is a messy and tricky area in
need of some attention from statisticians"*
– Britain in Numbers by Simon Briscoe

These are all current rates – e.g. Doesn't count
if you were *once* unemployed.

**Employee (even one hour a week
counts!):** 1 in 2
Part-time employed: 1 in 5
Self-employed: 1 in 10
Unemployed (looking for work): 1 in 20
**Inactive and not looking for work (disabled/
students/home carers and others):**
1 in 3
**Never held paid employment
(not including unpaid family workers
and students):** 1 in 25

**Never held paid employment
(including unpaid family workers and
students):**
1 in 6

Hold two jobs: 1 in 20
Retired: 1 in 5

Occupations

Acting: 1 in 1,000 (though many are
     'resting')
    Film: 1 in 15,000
    TV: 1 in 3,000
    Theatre: 1 in 2,000
    Walk-ons: 1 in 10,000
    Commercials: 1 in 2,000

Agricultural Worker: 1 in 200
Antique Dealer (not bric-a-brac shops!):
1 in 5,000
Architect: 1 in 1,500
Armed Forces – currently (ever):
    Officers: 1 in 2,000 (1 in 600)
    Other ranks: 1 in 200 (1 in 60)

Airline Pilot: 1 in 2,000
Auctioneer: 1 in 7,000
Banking and Accountancy: 1 in 25
Chartered Accountants: 1 in 250

'Bin Man': 1 in 300
Butler: 1 in 500 (mostly men!)
'Nanny': 1 in 250 (women)
Bar Staff: 1 in 100
Pub Landlord/lady/manager: 1 in 600
Master Baker: 1 in 10,000
Master Butcher: 1 in 5,000
Cartographer (mapmaker): 1 in 2,500
Candlestickmakers: ???

Chimney Sweep: 1 in 3,000 men
(1 in 20,000,000 women)
Thatcher: 1 in 700
Church Ministers: 1 in 1,200
Circus/street performer: 1 in 1,000
Magician (Magic Circle): 1 in 15,000 men
(1 in 200,000 women)
Fairground Show person: 1 in 1,000
Construction: 1 in 20 and decreasing in
many areas
Steelwork: 1 in 1,500 currently (1 in 150
ever)
Ship Building: 1 in 2,500 currently
(1 in 250 ever)

Business/Computing/IT: 1 in 6
Engineer (member of Professional body):
1 in 250
Estate Agent: 1 in 300
Education: 1 in 11
    Teacher: 1 in 100
    Headteacher: 1 in 1,500
    University Lecturer: 1 in 1,000
    'Dinner Lady': 1 in 250

Fishing Industry: 1 in 2,500 men

Health and Social Services: 1 in 6
    NHS only: 1 in 30
    Doctor: 1 in 500 of which:
    Consultant: 1 in 1,500
    GP: 1 in 1,000
    Nurse: 1 in 50 women (1 in 500 men)

Dentist: 1 in 2,500
Midwife: 1 in 750
Cosmetic Surgeon: 1 in 10,000
Optician: 1 in 5,000
Pharmacist: 1 in 1,000
Paramedic: 1 in 500
Hypnotherapist: 1 in 40,000

Landscape gardener: 1 in 1,500
Hairdresser/barber/beauty specialist:
1 in 300

Any Service industry: Only 1 in 3 are not!

The 'Media'
Presenter/broadcaster/journalist -
  TV: 1 in 3,000
  Radio: 1 in 1,000
  Newspapers: 1 in 1,000

National Trust volunteer: 1 in 10,000

RNLI crew member: 1 in 1,000
(1 in 15,000 women)

General Sports Industry: 1 in 50

Wholesale/Retailing: 1 in 5

Hotel/restaurants: 1 in 14
  Chef: 1 in 300
  Sous chef/Cook: 1 in 50
  Waiter: 1 in 20

Legal Service
   Barrister: 1 in 2,000
   'Silk' (Queen's Counsel): 1 in 20,000
   Solicitor: 1 in 500
   Magistrate: 1 in 2,000
   Judge: 1 in 10,000

Librarian: 1 in 1,500
Manufacturing: 1 in 7
Mining: 1 in 2,500 men currently and decreasing (1 in 200 ever)
Merchant Navy: 1 in 1,500
   Officer: 1 in 2,000
   Rating: 1 in 3,000

**Motor Vehicle mechanic
(one who can do anything, not just bodywork bashing!):** 1 in 1,000

Driving Instructor: 1 in 1,500
Taxi Drivers (licenced Hackney only): 1 in 300
Professional Driver – HGV or PSV: 1 in 20

Police: 1 in 300
   Inspector and above: 1 in 4,000

Fireman/woman: 1 in 1,500
Traffic Warden: 1 in 1,500

Piano Tuners: 1 in 400

Prostitute: 1 in 1,000 (women)

Stripper/lap/pole-dancer: 1 in 500 women
(1 in 10,000 men)

Public Administration: 1 in 15
   Civil Service: 1 in 100
   District/County councillor: 1 in 500
   Member of Parliament: 1 in 20,000

Surveyor: 1 in 500
Professional Writer/Poet: 1 in 1,000
Veterinary Surgeon: 1 in 2,000
Transport Worker: 1 in 16
Train Driver/crew: 1 in 1,500
'White Van' driver: 1 in 50
Printer: 1 in 200
Certified Plumber: 1 in 250

Post Office/Telecommunications Worker:
1 in 50

Call Centre Employee: 1 in 100
(could be much higher factor soon if
jobs move offshore)

How to improve your Memberships, Employment & Occupations Uniqueness Factor

Membership of a club or organisation – while some are more selective than others – is often a case of being prepared to pay the subscription fee. Be warned. On the other hand others are a prerequisite of professional acceptance and require years of experience and training, not to mention hard work.

Many of the rarer occupations (fishing, steel, coal mining) are a result of shrinkage of the industry and are hardly likely to offer fruitful employment – anyway it is not always advisable to focus on rare careers but if you are really considering 'downsizing' you might give these a thought:

The training required might be a little off-putting, but qualified 'butchers, bakers and candlestick makers' are all in pretty short supply, not to mention thatchers, sweeps and piano tuners!

You could simply get a second job...

PERSONAL LOG FOR MEMBERSHIPS, EMPLOYMENT AND OCCUPATIONS

Categories	Likelihood
Occupation:	
_____	_____
_____	_____
_____	_____
Memberships:	
_____	_____
_____	_____
_____	_____
New Categories:	
_____	_____
_____	_____
Estimated Likelihood	[ ]

Jamie Oliver

Has two children
(Poppy Honey & Daisy Boo):
1 in 3
Had book published: 1 in 500
Plays the drums: 1 in 40
Rides a motorcycle: 1 in 25
Has been to Australasia: 1 in 40

Uniqueness Factor

................in..........................

Sir David Jason

Married: 1 in 2
And he had been knighted just the day before!: 1
in 12,000
Scuba dives: 1 in 500
Flies gliders: 1 in 1,000
Had twin brother (who died at birth):
1 in 40

Uniqueness Factor

................in..........................

David Beckham

Blond hair: 1 in 3
More than two (three) children: 1 in 15
Plays golf: 1 in 20
Had book published: 1 in 500
Blue Peter Badge: 1 in 100

Uniqueness Factor

................in...........................

Lord Coe (Sebastian)

Member of House of Lords: 1 in 4,000
BSc degree: 1 in 6
More than two (four) children: 1 in 15
Likes the theatre (and never comes late?):
1 in 4
Likes live jazz: 1 in 7

Uniqueness Factor

................in...........................

Meeting Famous People

A few words of warning for this potentially quite personal section. Firstly – what is a 'celebrity'? Secondly – what counts as 'meeting' one?

Difficult questions when we all have rather different perceptions of what 'celebrity' means.

A working definition of 'celebrity' for the purposes of this book will be: "A celebrity is someone who is familiar to rather more people than they are personally acquainted with". (Still open to some debate but it's a start.)

As for 'meeting one', there are various levels, as you will see below.

In short this section should be taken with a little more than the usual amount of salt – but you still want to know your 'score', right?

Meeting a famous Celebrity (of TV / Film / Sports / whatever):

> **Do *not* have any famous person's autograph:**
> 1 in 4

(so now that is out of the way let's get down to the serious business)

> **Saw the person 'live' but after having paid for the privilege:** 1 in 1
> – almost everyone has been to a sports event or music concert at some time or another so this has zero effect on your UF

Saw the person 'live' while involved in some day to day activity such as shopping, dining, crossing the road or getting into a taxi: 1 in 5

Spoke to them (whether this was a welcome intrusion or not – brave chap!): 1 in 10

Have a photo of you with them: 1 in 50
(but this is getting easier all the time with camera phones)

Were introduced to them by a third party (aha, now we're getting somewhere):
1 in 100

Had coffee/lunch/a beer with: 1 in 200

Have been to the person's home: 1 in 500

They have been to your home: 1 in 1,000

More than the above....Wow!

Stalked a celebrity: This is a crime and if caught you will achieve an unwanted 'Crime and Theft' category score.

And specifically concerning 'Royalty':

Have attended a Royal Garden Party: 1 in 200
   Met Her Majesty the Queen: 1 in 300
   Met other 'Royal': 1 in 200
   Married one: 1 in 1,000,000!

My Pets

Have any Pet: 1 in 2

Owner of -
  Horse: 1 in 100
  Cat: 1 in 7
  Dog: 1 in 6
  Bird: 1 in 30
  Fish: 1 in 4
  Rabbit/Hamster/Guinea Pig/Gerbil:
  1 in 10
  (most of these tend to belong to children however)

Exotic pet (snake/spider): 1 in 250
If you have one that is legal and have taken professional advice on its care – you are to be highly commended. Most are illegal, badly cared for and could result in you being locked up – see crime!

Named your dog after a footballer: 1 in 10

Own a Dalmatian: 1 in 1,000 – why this one dog? Because it is the stupidest, most in-bred and often has *Heterochromia Iridium* (see Biological Self).

How to improve your Famous People and Pets Uniqueness Factor

Join the Armed Forces to meet a young Royal.

Start attending horsey events.

Simply move to London where every Hampstead or Notting Hill café is full of celebrities.

Become one of the hated paparazzi!

Or just stalk someone (and get into the Crime section too).

Alternatively, attendance at enough cultural and artistic events and regular participation in many of the things to be found in this book might well lead to an increased chance of being in the right place at the right time.

You might just become a celebrity yourself if you have sufficient interesting experiences – please credit this book if possible!

As for Pets – be careful what you buy and remember 'a puppy is not just for Christmas'…

PERSONAL LOG FOR FAMOUS PEOPLE AND MY PETS

Categories	Likelihood
People I've Met:	
_____	_____
_____	_____
_____	_____
Pets I Own:	
_____	_____
_____	_____
New Categories:	
_____	_____
_____	_____
Estimated Likelihood	☐

Ian Botham

Enjoys shooting: 1 in 125
And fishing: 1 in 50
Flies private aircraft: 1 in 1,000
Has acted regularly (in pantomime): 1 in 50
Has been south of the equator to Australia
(beating the Aussies!): 1 in 40

Uniqueness Factor

................in.........................

And for your interest –
he still manages to go on lots of Charity walks

Nick Faldo

Flies helicopters: 1 in 10,000
More than two (three) children: 1 in 15
Fishing: 1 in 50
Photography: 1 in 15
Woodworking: 1 in 50

Uniqueness Factor

................in.........................

House and Home

Type of Occupant –
 Owner (paid up): 1 in 3
 Owner (mortgage): 1 in 2 or 3 (actually 2 in 5)
 Renter: 1 in 3
 Free Accommodation: 1 in 1,000
 (e.g. pub landlords)

Type of house occupied –
 Flat/maisonette: 1 in 6
 Semi-detached: 1 in 3
 Detached: 1 in 5
 Bungalow: 1 in 40
 Terraced: 1 in 4
 Listed Building: 1 in 100
 Grade 1: 1 in 1,000

 Pre 1900: 1 in 10
 Farmhouse: 1 in 500
 Old converted school house: 1 in 5,000
 Old converted (and deconsecrated!) Church: 1 in 20,000
 Has thatched roof: 1 in 400

Haunted: 1 in 10,000 – now don't use this unless you are absolutely positive! Like you had a chat with it!

Live aboard a boat: 1 in 400
Public House: 1 in 1,000

With no yard or garden: 1 in 10

Valued at over 1 million pounds: 1 in 500 and decreasing!

Have moved home to be in a better school catchment area: 1 in 8

And you lucky second home owners!
    In the United Kingdom: 1 in 200
    In Europe: 1 in 200
    In USA: 1 in 2,000
    Other: 1 in 400
    Own a Timeshare apartment: 1 in 50
    And want to sell it: 1 in 100 (ie half of all owners!)

Possessions

You Do Have –

More than 30 ties: 1 in 10 men
Only black & white TV: 1 in 1,000
3 TVs or more: 1 in 4
5 TVs or more: 1 in 10
Digital camera: 1 in 10
Laptop computer: 1 in 10
Internet access (which was first used in 1989): 1 in 2
And Broadband: 1 in 3

And you still have an old Hi-Fi/turntable: 1 in 5
Or even better – reel to reel tape recorder: 1 in 25

You Do Not Have –

PC: 1 in 2
CD player: 1 in 8
Mobile phone (Did you know the first was in 1973?): 1 in 3
Any landline phone: 1 in 20
TV: 1 in 100
DVD: 1 in 3

How to improve your House & Home and Possessions Uniqueness Factor

These days this is more easily said than done – more and more first time buyers are struggling to get any kind of foothold on the property ladder – just hope the property bubble doesn't burst at the wrong time…

Rather than be an 'early adopter' always trying – in vain – to "keep up with the Jones's" why not hang on to the old stuff and become an eccentric – and get an ever higher UF? Hoarding all kinds of stuff indiscriminately will make collecting anything in particular seem far less of a chore. After all, pretty soon even a video tape player will be a rarity, not to mention that old SLR camera.

Personal Log for House & Home and Possessions

Categories	Likelihood
My Home in All Its Splendour	
_____	_____
_____	_____
_____	_____
_____	_____
_____	_____
_____	_____
New Categories:	
_____	_____
_____	_____
Estimated Likelihood	[ ]

Crime and Theft

I have kept this brief as it could be rather off-putting – still people might just want to know!
[Due to problems of accurately recording and defining crimes 'within the last year only' statistics are given unless otherwise specified]

> **You were the Victim**
>> **Any crime:** 1 in 4
>> **Mugged:** 1 in 150
>> **Any violence:** 1 in 20
>> **Burgled:** 1 in 30
>> **Car stolen:** 1 in 125
>> **Bicycle stolen:** 1 in 100
>> (worst in Cambridge! 10 per day!)
> **Victim more than once in last year:** 1 in 15
>
> **You were the criminal!**
>> **Were merely cautioned:** 1 in 500
>> **Actually were sentenced to prison:** 1 in 300. But approximately 1 in 50 men (1 in 500 women) have ever been convicted and sent to prison
>> **Prisoner (at time of reading this book!):** 1 in 600
>> **Soliciting prostitute:** 1 in 15,000
>> (almost always by a man)
>> **Theft from the Royal Mail:** 1 in 3,000
>> **Drug use:** 1 in 1,000
>> **Speeding fine (in last three years):** 1 in 11
>> **Breathalysed (in last three years):** 1 in 14

How to improve your Crime & Theft Uniqueness Factor

The safest action might appear to be to remain at home (most burglaries occur when the property is vacant) but this precludes achieving all those other interesting things you want to do, so why not buy a hi-tech security system and get on with your life.

You might also want to consider taking a self defence/martial arts course (see Sports), driving carefully and…basically just remember…

**Don't do anything illegal
however attractive it might appear at first!**

PERSONAL LOG FOR CRIME & THEFT

Categories	Likelihood
Crimes Suffered as Victim:	
_____	_____
_____	_____
_____	_____
_____	_____
Crimes Committed:	
_____	_____
_____	_____
New Categories:	
_____	_____
_____	_____
Estimated Likelihood	

Paula Radcliffe

Married: 1 in 2
Blonde haired: 1 in 3
Been to USA
(won New York and Chicago Marathons!):
1 in 15
Been south of equator: 1 in 15
Enjoys reading: 1 in 2

Uniqueness Factor
................in...........................

Sir Steve Redgrave

Married: 1 in 2
6'5 1/4" tall: 1 in 100
Book published: 1 in 500
Been south of equator: 1 in 15
Winter Sports
(Former national Bobsleigh champion!):
1 in 20

Uniqueness Factor
................in...........................

Wealth and Income

Income (pre tax!) and Liquid Assets*:

No savings at all: 1 in 4
Shares – hold some: 1 in 6
Earn less than £7,000 pa: 1 in 10
Have 'liquid assets' of at least £10,000:
    1 in 5
Earning more than £40,000 pa: 1 in 10
**Earn more than £50,000 pa or have more
than £150,000 in 'liquid assets':** 1 in 20
**Earn more than £120,000 pa or have more
than £700,000 in 'liquid assets':** 1 in 100
**Have more than £7 million in 'liquid
assets':** 1 in 300
**Have more than £70 million in 'liquid
assets':** 1 in 40,000

** 'liquid assets' mean all your savings and
investments but excluding your own home!*

Savings and Debt:
    At least 4 credit/debit cards: 1 in 2
    No credit card: 1 in 3

    **Have a debt of some kind other than a
    mortgage:** 1 in 2
    Have ever been declared bankrupt:
    1 in 150

In serious debt (over £10,000 pounds):
   1 in 20

Savings over £10,000: 1 in 5
No savings at all: 1 in 4
No current bank account: 1 in 10

Have a loan of some kind: 1 in 7

And remember – most of these should not
be combined

And just to see how altruistic you can be
with all this money…

Donated to charity in last year
   (at least £5 cheapskate!): 1 in 2
   but gave more than £50: 1 in 20

Family Life

Married: 1 in 2
Never married: 1 in 3
Divorced: 1 in 10
Widowed: 1 in 15

Children:
None: 1 in 3
One or Two: 1 in 3
More than Two: 1 in 15

Mother of:
Twins: 1 in 100
Triplets: 1 in 6,000
Quads or more! : 1 in 300,000

Prefer to have a 'home birth':
1 in 50 (women!)

Vegetarian: 1 in 30

How to improve your Wealth & Income and Family Life Uniqueness Factor

Fewer and fewer people are getting married. More and more are living at home until they do, so that visit to the clinic for 'fertility research' might well come in doubly useful at this stage, not least as it might also result in more debt, push you on to the property ladder and make you hang on to all those items you were meaning to throw away. Of course if you live long enough everything will change when all your children look after you in the manner to which you wish to be accustomed.

PERSONAL LOG FOR WEALTH & INCOME AND FAMILY LIFE

Categories	Likelihood
Income:	
_____	_____
_____	_____
Savings:	
_____	_____
_____	_____
Family Circumstances:	
_____	_____
_____	_____
New Categories:	
_____	_____
Estimated Likelihood	[ ]

Health and Physical Attributes

MISCELLANEOUS!

Unfit to serve in the military (16 to 55 years old): 1 in 6
Currently/recently dieting: 1 in 4
(1 in 3 women)
Use the 'pill': 1 in 4 (women)
Eat health food: 1 in 4
Visit coffee bar: 1 in 25
Smoke: 1 in 4
Snore: 1 in 3
Stutter: 1 in 100
Are obese : BMI (Kg + height in metres^2) is equal to or greater than 30) : 1 in 4
Have private healthcare: 1 in 10
Have a tattoo/piercing: 1 in 10
Don't use suncream: 1 in 4
Have ever taken part in clinical drug trials: 1 in 50
Had face lift:
    Women: 1 in 50
    Men: 1 in 500

LONG TERM AILMENTS
(Things you still have...)

Allergies: 1 in 3
Asthma: 1 in 12
Suffer from mental illness
  Mild: 1 in 6
  Severe: 1 in 50
Sleepwalking (somnambulism): 1 in 25
Autism: 1 in 150
ADHD: 1 in 25
Crohn's disease/colitis (IBD - Inflammatory bowel disorder) 1 in 300
King Alfred the Great and founder of England as we know it was thought to have been a sufferer)

Irritable bowel syndrome (IBS): 1 in 20
(this must not be confused with the much rarer and more serious IBD)
Dyslexia: 1 in 6
Eating disorders: 1 in 100 women (1 in 1,000 men)
Epilepsy: 1 in 200 (Elton John is a sufferer)
Multiple Sclerosis: 1 in 1,000
Repetitive strain injury (RSI): 1 in 50
Tourette's syndrome: 1 in 2,000

PHOBIAS

Any: 1 in 10
Acrophobia: (fear of heights): 1 in 25
Agoraphobia (fear of open spaces): 1 in 80
(Kim Basinger, actress)

Claustrophobia: 1 in 50
Social phobia (public speaking): 1 in 50
Obsessive Compulsive Disorder (OCD –
this commonly manifests as repetitive actions
which disrupt the sufferer's normal life such
as cleaning of the same area over and over):
1 in 80
Aviatophobia (fear of flying!): 1 in 15
(Glenda Jackson, Dennis Bergkamp)

THE SENSES

Hearing
    Any Problems: 1 in 6
    Hearing Aid: 1 in 25
    Tinnitus: 1 in 7

Eyesight
    Wear Spectacles: 1 in 2
    Short sighted (myopic): 1 in 3
    Long sighted (hyperopic): 1 in 3

    Have had laser eye treatment: 1 in 10,000
    Wear Contact lenses: 1 in 15
    Heterochromia Iridium (genetically
    different coloured eyes): 1 in 1,000

Colour Blindness –
    Red/Green: 1 in 8 men (1 in 200 women)
    Total (Achromatopsia): 1 in 30,000
    men/women equal – for a change!

Dental Health
Grind teeth: 1 in 5
Have most of original untreated teeth:
1 in 2 (but drops to 1 in 5 after 45!)
Have no teeth: 1 in 10 (Ok this too is
highly biased against older folk!)
Wear dentures: 1 in 5 (ditto!)

Drinking Habits
Heavily (this much on at least one day in
the week – remember one unit is half a pint
of beer, a glass of wine or a single spirit
measure)
(more than 8 units per day men): 1 in 4
(more than 6 units per day women)
1 in 10
You claim to be teetotal: 1 in 6!!

ILLNESSES SUFFERED

Major Illnesses or Operations:
Cancer: 1 in 50
Heart disease: 1 in 100
Stroke: 1 in 300
Flu/pneumonia: 1 in 70
Hip fracture: 1 in 20

Admitted to hospital due to -
And remember these figures are all for adults only!

Collision with a cyclist: 1 in 6,000

So if you want to raise your score several times, move to Cambridge where not only are there more bicycles than anywhere else in the UK, hence more chance of being hit by one, but you have a greater chance of yours being stolen too! (see thefts)

Falling off bike: 1 in 200
Falling on snow or ice: 1 in 400
Falling from skates: 1 in 500
Falling from a tree: 1 in 2,000
Injured by firework: 1 in 10,000

NB So it's easy to see how to up the score here – act like a kid!!

Then again…

Injured by lawnmower: 1 in 3,000
Injured by a non-powered tool
   (e.g. garden rake, hammer): 1 in 250
Suffered 'hot drink' injury: 1 in 2,000
Came off worst in interaction with kitchen
   appliance (e.g. kettle, iron): 1 in 2,000
Cut or 'stabbed' yourself(!): 1 in 200

Victim of Flood, Storm, Avalanche,
Earthquake or Volcanic Eruption: 1 in 20,000
Struck by Lightning: 1 in 25,000
Were (un)fortunate enough to have object
left inside you after an operation:
1 in 10,000

Suffered injury by impacting sporting equipment: 1 in 400
Suffered sporting injury specifically involving a collision with another player: 1 in 500 (Jonny Wilkinson, amongst many other sports players)

Were Bitten by:
   Person: 1 in 1,000
   Dog: 1 in 600
   Other animal (including rats, alligators, crocodiles, scorpions, spiders and sharks!): 1 in 600

And a final reminder, these data are for admissions to a hospital.

Many people simply don't need, or choose, to admit themselves after experiencing similar events; so to score highly, go to hospital – just try to avoid catching an infection while there, unlike the unfortunate minority of 1 in 10 in-patients.

But honestly do you really want to 'improve' your health score on this section?

Fair enough! There just might be a few ways to up the UF without subjecting your body to pain and injury – treating yourself to private medical care is no bad way to begin in the current climate and laser eye treatment is gaining in popularity (but there seem to be lots of very rich people with poor eyesight who don't appear to have had it done...yet).

Otherwise I think this is another category where being less special actually helps.

PERSONAL LOG FOR HEALTH & PHYSICAL ATTRIBUTES

Categories	Likelihood
Miscellaneous:	
Illnesses/Ailments:	
Phobias:	
Senses Hearing:	
Sight:	
Teeth:	
Injuries Suffered/Hospital Admissions:	
New Categories:	
Estimated Likelihood	

Anna Ford

Has (two) children: 1 in 3
Holds BA Degree: 1 in 6
Was an Open University tutor: 1 in 1,000
Likes gardening: 1 in 2
And drawing: 1 in 10

Uniqueness Factor

................in...........................

Sir Elton John

Plays tennis: 1 in 50
Gay (re-married in civil partnership): 1 in 12
Legally changed name
(from Reginald Kenneth Dwight – to Elton
Hercules John – after the Steptoe & Son horse!):
1 in 5,000
Epileptic: 1 in 200
Has had a pacemaker fitted: 1 in 100

Uniqueness Factor

................in...........................

Sir Jimmy Savile

Single (never married): 1 in 3
Runs: 1 in 200
Cycles: 1 in 10
Wrestles: 1 in 300
Does (lots of) charity walks: 1 in 60

Uniqueness Factor

................in...........................

Dame Helen Mirren

Blonde hair: 1 in 3
Used to work at an amusement park
attracting people onto rollercoaster!
(Circus/fairgrounds): 1 in 1,000
Been to Russia
(born of Russian aristocratic family): 1 in 250
Changed name (from Ilynea Lydia Mironoff):
1 in 50

Uniqueness Factor

................in...........................

Awards, Titles and Medals

Anything at all (trophy/certificate/plaque) for winning / coming runner-up or just 'being in it'! (Fun runs are a great way to get these!): 1 in 3

Blue Peter badges: 1 in 100 – mostly Blue or Green – you have Gold? Wow!!): (Jonny Wilkinson, David Beckham, Patrick Moore)

Duke of Edinburgh's award:
    All awards: 1 in 40
    But the Gold: 1 in 500

First Aid: 1 in 50 (Red Cross, St John's Ambulance or Royal Life Saving Society mainly)

Nobel prize: 1 in 5,000,000

Victoria Cross (military bravery): 1 in 3,000,000

George Cross (civilian bravery): 1 in 2,000,000

Any of Companion/Officer or Member of the order of the British Empire:
1 in 500 or specifically -
   CBE: 1 in 5,000
   OBE: 1 in 2,500
   MBE: 1 in 1,000

People who have rejected their awards:
1 in 10,000 (most of these are not made public due to the nature of the protocol surrounding the awards)

All members of Aristocracy NOT including spouse/children – BUT including both Hereditary and Life Peers: 1 in 15,000

And the Order of Precedence from the highest (should you need to be even more specific)

Duke/Duchess
Marquess/Marchioness
Earl/Countess
Viscount/ess
Baron/ess

Membership of each individual class is relatively rare but 'slightly' less so is the class of **Baronet/ess**: 1 in 20,000

Knight/Dame: 1 in 12,000 (according to the Chancery of Knighthood) but this includes all rankings – there are fewer than 1,000 in the restricted orders (Garter, Thistle, Bath etc) which would make their holders 1 in 50,000

How to improve your Awards, Titles & Medals Uniqueness Factor

At the simplest level, go and participate in just about anything! Lots of ordinary people get an honour of some kind but it tends to take a long time and not being afraid to put your head above the parapet a bit!

You could simply (!) marry into the aristocracy and a woman would be at the very least 'Lady so-and-so'; though a man would not generally acquire any title (marrying a Queen is slightly different!). Children can inherit titles – but not within the modern Life Peerages – so leave this book in your will!

Otherwise you'll just need to work your way up the ladder of lesser awards until you receive the knighthood!

Many of the others need a lot of inspiration (this book?!) and effort – but the score is well worth it!

Religion

Christian of any denomination:
more than 1 in 2

Anglican: 1 in 2
Roman Catholic: 1 in 6
Methodist: 1 in 70
Presbyterian: 1 in 70
Baptised (any denomination): 1 in 7

Muslim 1 in 30
Hindu: 1 in 100
Sikh: 1 in 150
Jewish: 1 in 200
Buddhist: 1 in 300
Mormon: 1 in 300
Other: (including Jedi Knight at the last census):
1 in 300

No declared religion: 1 in 5
(All of the above are according to self-declaration
– this is not meant to indicate any level of
commitment – for that however....

Never attend any place of worship: 1 in 3

Regularly attend Sunday Church: 1 in 12

PERSONAL LOG FOR AWARDS, TITLES & MEDALS, RELIGION

Categories	Likelihood
Awards & Medals Held:	
My Title:	
My Religious Belief:	
New Categories:	
Estimated Likelihood	

MY SELF

My Best Five Categories:

....

One in ....

....

One in ....

....

One in ....

....

One in ....

....

One in ....

My Uniqueness Factor Calculation:

................in...........................

MY SPOUSE/PARTNER

Best Five Categories:

....

One in ....

....

One in ....

....

One in ....

....

One in ....

....

One in ....

His/Her Uniqueness Factor Calculation:

................in...........................

My Best Friend

Best Five Categories:

....

One in ....

....

One in ....

....

One in ....

....

One in ....

....

One in ....

Uniqueness Factor Calculation:

...............in...........................

My [other relative/friend]

Best Five Categories:

....

One in ....

....

One in ....

....

One in ....

....

One in ....

....

One in ....

Uniqueness Factor Calculation:

................in...........................

How to complete a
Certificate of Achievement *(facing page)*

It is Hereby Declared that

[insert your name here]
....

Is Quite Possibly

One in Only *[insert your UF here]*
....

Of the Adult Population
of the United Kingdom Who

1............*Has/is/plays*

2............*Has/is/plays*

3.........................

4.........................

And

5.........................

Signed
[your own signature here]

Certificate of Achievement

It is Hereby Declared that

....

Is Quite Possibly

One in Only ....

Of the Adult Population
of the United Kingdom Who

1..........................

2.......................

3.......................

4.......................

And

5.......................

Signed

References

The data contained in this book is a combination of estimation, derivation, extrapolation, comparison and very occasionally simple conversion (from a percentage or fraction) to obtain a probability based on the author's own reasonable judgement of the most relevant United Kingdom adult population cohort for the value in question. In this respect it is highly unlikely that any one of the many and varied sources consulted by the author provided the information necessary to derive any of the vast majority of the values contained herein, nor is it possible to point the reader straight towards the source for direct confirmation. Nevertheless the following were found to be consistently valuable sources from which probability values were ultimately created: The Office for National Statistics (including but not limited to National Census data, 'Social Trends', 'Travel Trends', General Household Survey, 'British Crime Survey', 'Hospital Episodes', 'International Passenger Survey' data), The Departments of the Deputy Prime Minister, Transport, Education and Science, Culture, Media and Sport, The English Tourism Council, The National Tourist Boards, United Kingdom Tourism Survey, Sport England. In addition I am particularly grateful for the inspiration I obtained from reading such publications as "Britain In Numbers: the essential statistics", (Simon Briscoe – Politico's), "101 Things to Do Before You Die", (Richard Horne – Bloomsbury) and 100 Things to Do Before You Die (New Scientist Profile).

Except where otherwise acknowledged, the information included in this work is believed to be 'common knowledge' and its sources are many and varied. Whilst there has been no verbatim use of copy I am also indebted to "Who's Who (A&C Black), "Debrett's People of Today" (Debrett's Peerage) and many National Governing Bodies and organisations for the information gleaned from their websites or in answer to my enquiries. And finally without the Office for National Statistics much of the information I have used would have been far more difficult to obtain.

Acknowledgements

Many thanks to all the people who contributed in any way to this book – especially those who replied promptly to my enquiries for data and the select few who actually suggested content or made useful comments on the drafts: Pete S, Cliff Y, Gary B, Ian G, Donna, Paul W, and Nick F.